A Drip-Drop in a Tea Shop

by Spencer Brinker

Consultant:
Beth Gambro
Reading Specialist
Yorkville, Illinois

Contents

BEARPORT PUBLISHING

New York, New York

A Drip-Drop in a Tea Shop

Mrs. **Frop** has a tiny tea **shop**.

Inside the **shop**,
she can hear a
drip-**drop**.

The drips fill a cup,
spilling over the **top**.

The cup tips over with a very loud **plop**.

There's a splash on the floor next to a **mop**.

The **mop** falls over.

It hits a sleeping **cop**.

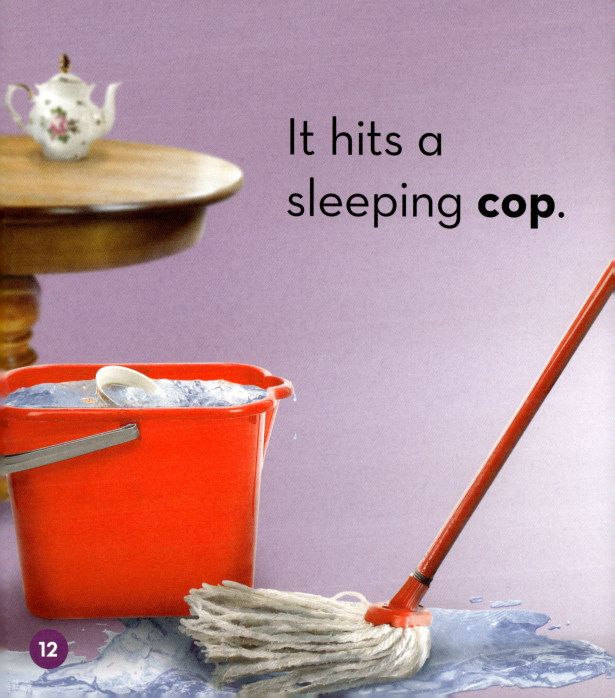

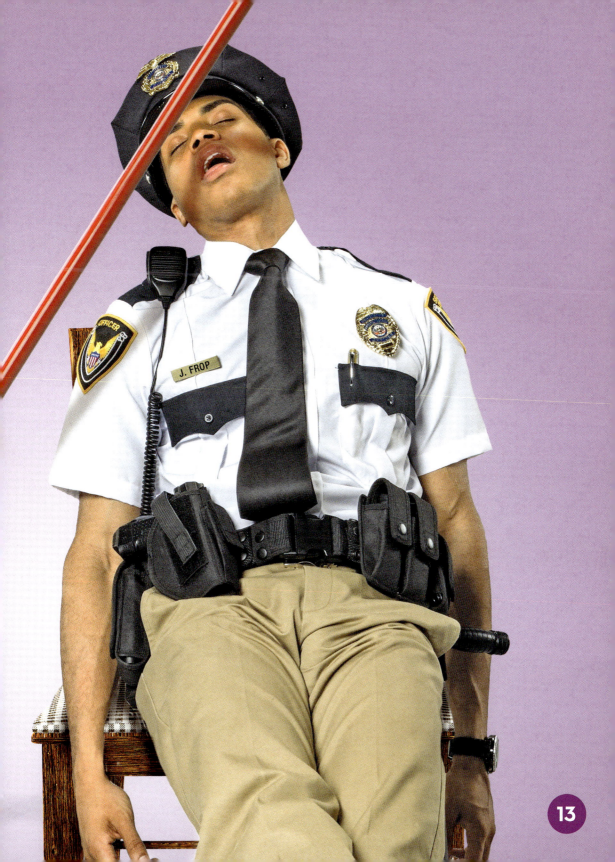

The **cop** jumps up.
He yells, "**Stop**!"

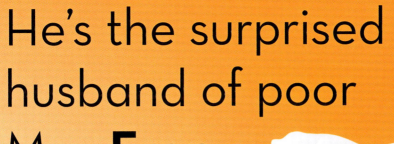

He's the surprised husband of poor Mrs. **Frop**.

Key Words in the -op Family

cop

drop

mop

plop

shop

stop

top

Other **-op** Words: **chop, flop, hop, pop**

Index

About the Author

Spencer Brinker loves to tell "dad jokes" and play word games with his twin girls.

Teaching Tips

Before Reading
- ✔ Introduce rhyming words and the **–op** word family to readers.
- ✔ Guide readers on a "picture walk" through the text by asking them to name the things shown.
- ✔ Discuss book structure by showing children where text will appear consistently on pages. Highlight the supportive pattern of the book.

During Reading
- ✔ Encourage readers to "read with your finger" and point to each word as it is read. Stop periodically to ask children to point to a specific word in the text.
- ✔ Reading strategies: When encountering unknown words, prompt readers with encouraging cues such as:
  - **Does that word look like a word you already know?**
  - **Does it rhyme with another word you have already read?**

After Reading
- ✔ Write the key words on index cards.
  - **Have readers match them to pictures in the book.**
- ✔ Ask readers to identify their favorite page in the book. Have them read that page aloud.
- ✔ Choose an **–op** word. Ask children to pick a word that rhymes with it.
- ✔ Ask children to create their own rhymes using **–op** words. Encourage them to use the same pattern found in the book.

Credits: Cover, © Sandratsky Dmitriy/Shutterstock and © gowithstock/Shutterstock; 2–3, © 9nong/Shutterstock and © vipman/Shutterstock; 4–5, © 9nong/Shutterstock, © Vadim Petrakov/Shutterstock, and © vipman/Shutterstock; 6–7, © movit/Shutterstock, © 5 second Studio/Shutterstock, © SeDmi/Shutterstock, © Shushan Harutyunyan/Shutterstock, © gowithstock/Shutterstock, and © Vadim Petrakov/Shutterstock; 8–9, © indigolotos/Shutterstock, © gowithstock/Shutterstock, and © Vadim Petrakov/Shutterstock; 10–11, © indigolotos/Shutterstock, © gowithstock/Shutterstock, and © Vadim Petrakov/Shutterstock; 12–13, © LifetimeStock/Shutterstock, © indigolotos/Shutterstock, © gowithstock/Shutterstock, and © Vadim Petrakov/Shutterstock; 14–15, © LifetimeStock/Shutterstock, © 9nong/Shutterstock, © indigolotos/Shutterstock, © Shushan Harutyunyan/Shutterstock, © movit/Shutterstock; 16T (L to R), © LifetimeStock/Shutterstock, © Claudio Divizia/Shutterstock, © indigolotos/Shutterstock, and © gowithstock/Shutterstock; 16B (L to R), © vipman/Shutterstock, © Kaspri/Shutterstock, and © Victeah/Shutterstock.

Publisher: Kenn Goin   **Senior Editor**: Joyce Tavolacci   **Creative Director**: Spencer Brinker

Library of Congress Cataloging-in-Publication Data: Names: Brinker, Spencer, author. | Gambro, Beth, consultant. Title: A drip-drop in a tea shop / by Spencer Brinker; consultant: Beth Gambro, Reading Specialist, Yorkville, Illinois. Description: New York, New York: Bearport Publishing, [2020] | Series: Read and rhyme: Level 3 | Includes index. Identifiers: LCCN 2019007176 (print) | LCCN 2019012631 (ebook) | ISBN 9781642806168 (Ebook) | ISBN 9781642805628 (library) | ISBN 9781642807202 (pbk.) Subjects: LCSH: Readers (Primary) Classification: LCC PE1119 (ebook) | LCC PE1119 .B751835 2020 (print) | DDC 428.6/2–dc23 LC record available at https://lccn.loc.gov/2019007176

10 9 8 7 6 5 4 3 2 1